Finding Ft. George

for Cindy

Finding
Ft. George

Rob Budde

Dec/07

CAITLIN PRESS

Caitlin Press
Distributed by Harbour Publishing
PO Box 219
Madeira Park, BC, Canada V0N 2H0
www.caitlin-press.com

Cover design by Anna Comfort
Cover photographs of Prince George beehive burner
    by James Girouard
Printed and bound in Canada

Library and Archives Canada Cataloguing in Publication

Budde, Robert, 1966–
    Finding Ft. George / Rob Budde.

Poems.
ISBN 978-1-894759-27-4

    I. Title.

PS8553.U446F46 2007   C813'.6   C2007-903883-2

for pg

contents

I

finding ft. george

finding ft. george

dear pg/1

river cottonwood esker versus sky behind
sun shook, shimmered

greens (the trees wonder
    how long we've been here)

verse an imprint, the passage of
human hands/ i
stood reading local history, the river
changed, my eyes diverted/ i
changed

a record of sap, stills, sluice,
smoke lifting, sagging into breath-
less endeavors/ i
walk farther
read further ...

dear pg/2

    barry playing drums i thot jazz tho i was tired and he
looking sternly amused, cool, at the other poet, stories
of leather pants propositioned in front of the ramada (the
hollywood casino no less)(now empty)
    i was house hunting (sans 30/30) told the bowl stunk
all the profs live in the hart (misheard as *heart*—wow, such
passion, i thot) up above the smell. the place a real estate
economy first, even as i tried to look around. the campus

perched there above the swell of pulp-mill exhalations and beer swilling. the money rises.

a gunslinger that's what he looked like barry with a precise grey moustache, sharp features, the quick eyes—barry the gunslinger wanting time, poems, no show/downs

across the 3rd ave. bar hours to get a beer after a set, "i've been hired in creative writing at unbc." i think *writing* and *unbc* register, barry unmoved "great, great" (me reading, "yeah, whatever") that point when we know a person might be passing through, no register, why work at it

barry's book in my packsack

and not,
just like barry

when i saw the downtown it was familiar. any resource town would know it. the ones i knew—yellowknife, thompson, sault ste. marie—all conjured by the '70s-style awning, the boarded-up windows, the lack of pretense in landscaping, the new big boxes on the outskirts scooping up what fiscal agility the town has left (their taxes waved, the town waving bye-bye)

hello prince george, pleased to meet you

a few months later barry and i at the BX after many emails. *cagey* is what i thot, cautious, like he'd been assaulted in a similar situation, smacked by the trap of collegiality

such dignity—he's a poetry statesman

he drinks .5% beer (not now, but then, talks about drinking as if to fend off demons) quietly explaining history and the hovering threat of alcoholism like an administrative squeeze. we're all up against it

over his stories, the writers' disease, suknaski gone mad

the BX paddlewheel motif a mystery until someone tells

12

me the boats used to go up and down the fraser (why not now?), the historying begun

the new casino going up behind mr. pg (do you think he'll get a cut?) called "treasure cove" no less. dealers as usual and the trees swept aside

words, signs, a poetic history—this is where capitalism sheds its skin

dear pg/3

purdy's cariboo horses aren't
here, really
he is, the beer and gruff
grasp on what it means
to have balls (barry says
he pulled that one)
or more

foley's cache, stewart names
the past, ft. george
the traces of settlement sediment
piling up to the big
houses in college heights and
the moonscape subdivisions
gargoyles of vinyl siding

back and forth history slides i
swing hearing stanley,
fawcett and thesen
creeley and the lines
highway and rail intersecting
river taking us all away

dear pg/4

ken built a house with his bare hands. everything. and
poems mean a lot to him. sound, rhythm, the reconfiguration
of language samples. this gives me hope

ken sends me love poems to steelhead trout. from the
alberta farm to 1960s vancouver east-side poets to long hair
in smithers to the dream of damdochax lake and then there.
all the way, out there.

how joists are made, how logs are fitted together, how
poets meet talk over carrot juice with si busy about and cats,
each a precise surface, a careful edge; this is where we live

he looks across the table: "the north is moving..."

dear pg/5

barry mugged in peru and hearing about shootings in la
paz. here and there—the assemblage retold. and i, reading
of the shooting over taxes and the police protesting (nothing
new under the sun?) in the *new internationalist* magazine. the
two accounts come across, cross, barry borrows the magazine.
i have his poem. information and the lovely vacuum of
knowing. we wander.

dear pg/6

on seething, offset:
what the outside insiders teach
is garrison, a kind of highway rage
without motion and no passing lane
a kind of stillness, shaking with

indignation without a source or socket
ratcheting up and poetry inches
out, an angular gesture to not
inquire, a manipulation of the surface
tension, spittle, and grit.

it's about leaving the cities. fully.
it's about leaving the lyric and the city's full
use of us.

what the inside outsiders teach
is male violence clamped to text, variations on
vehemence, a defensive posture
a small-business owner with a shotgun
language and bottle glasses—firing off into the woods
at wolves who've left at first whiff.

words like water cool the burner, even
off-rhythm eddies—the turn
in a moment's reflection stir.

pg is writing, worrying
over the line, what it is taking us for.

dear pg/7

i dreamt of this place six years
before i saw it for the first time;
cutbanks and evergreens, the draws
and eskers pliant to the industrial surge

i dreamt prince george before it was

fish flash, a brown hand, a willow basket

prince george like an ice dam, flotsam
caught against the jam of bush

you see them, deriding the cops, imbibing and
disdainful—the bush people, from outside yet
land and spirits are not so separable—
the undergrowth grows over, back
out beyond what we blueprinted

the tallest building in prince george
unlivable, watches smoke, the churning
of products through machines and mouths

nostalgia is the thoughts we have when nothing
else works

giving way

either living off the land or accruing debt;
different houses, same lives

a kind of slow leeching of nutrients
falling out of the language

I am obtrusive in cities because
I step aside, give way
and throw off everything

the colonial inclination to cohesion—writing
the good story—and
empty space a vision of development

yesterday, a strip mall ate my path
inside out

here, capitalist pretense falls
away like manners

policies are roads and I am off

"green" noun

what is inside saying a kind
of explosion of the singular

sound is unsound thought in a

word or located idea—
not both—across a table
but talk of how to stay
in language and land—
not both—across a poem its own

myth is the expectation
that some have done it for you better

causing knots of recoil, not taking what is given, not
beholden to the south—sustainability is

in poetics, is keeping the poem close,
a territory, a ceremony, a smaller economy
of naming ink into thought out

meaning can stay in catalogues,
the course lists, the collective
protections, a manifesto that is not one saying

prince george is not memorable
like that usual world.

the new subdivision

temporary roads & sewer
drain regulations materialize from
a specific place

a text trained to be
a discourse of progress—
the poem's paperwork crosses a desk

yet chalk outlines of the original
system persists in the half-light

levelled—the street name,
the name exists first
a kind of sluice where
the bylaw feeds to
highway, cars will start
the morning named automatic

*   *   *

the forgotten body
sprawls across the dirt access
road, limbs twisted—
a new kind of centrefold—
but there is evidence here, traces
available even after excavation
covers it all up
with the 6 o'clock
news' stocks

*   *   *

topography sheds responsibility,
ashes cast into
zones, the machine
at the break of green
belt blown over
the ornamental replacement

the bulldozer driver is
an editor   confident of his terrain,
and he leaves three trees out of every three
hundred, leaning,
then shocked a swimming pool
and its virtual horizons

        ❋ ❋ ❋

sod is trucked in
stacked in carpet rolls
on top of the remaining saplings,
thimbleberry and devil's club

    names shocked—
    the stalk's thorns
    re-inscribe

the subdivision is successful and
lots are sold in advance contracts;
"speculation" here is the gaze
of pornographers

the next book, the poetics
purchased by transient affluence

* * *

the poet bikes by
looking at the shape, the progress

air moves differently up the slope
water has begun to wash away the soil
cement basements commit suicide
and the underbrush
browns like an affidavit

> *perception moves, uses*
> *movement, shifts*
> *again to allow the form*
> *to evolve*

the title of the piece will be
a headline invented by a real estate agent
whose father abused him until he was fourteen
and his family name
on the community centre wall

civic plans
fan out, blueprints
from a stray
victim starting
to speak

the old road

discussion was inadequate,
it didn't move us—
that new language wasn't there
now or then

when inscriptions sank blood
and charters bloomed in the ditch
i was there, shining,
a bobble in the wet loam

parchment bark timed by
the traces of access
and construction, less
overgrown and constant
then the land could bear

edges, boundaries sunk
in, filled in, and then recut
with the scythe of pure politics

to distinguish but not name
or the reverse—the lichen
remained an impossible
feat heightened by loss
under the recurring suggestion
that this was once something
inhumane

inversions of faith
for P.G.

a high pressure press
the poetry of socked in and breathing hard

sunk, dumped on, and developing
symptoms, the air an irony;
worker's compensation sucked back

a microbrew fermenting versus
the trucked-in ad about a hick drinking—
identity a stupid trick of space

parts of speech a fine
particulate i assume daily, take it
on faith, wondering too
if eskers are real

the language of servitude is an aggressive one
piled up against the spare in the back

being used is an economic lever, fiscal pride spray-
painted in orange on the back of each load pried out

wooden blood, the arteries a single lane
bypass and seasonal pacemaker—seizing

but this is
about faith, about inhaling
and admitting it—
being here, looking up at the press of sky and
staying

the vibrant economy

the future
nurselog hauled

at least
a hundred

clicks
east dissembled

in the fingerboard plant—

oh, the astonished cinders

ends of the earth

toad licks her lips
slouches in the mooseprint
hoping the earth holds on

splitting kindling with a bad axe

It's a small motion but shipped in
from a long way off. The log is always
local but the iron old. Lines in the grain
work against the classic pose—you either
cohabitate or battle the common prose. I'm neither
here nor there but green like rooted wood. The handle
is key—a woodcutter taught me that
in 1741—for the feel of it, looking for the way
in, unforced, keen. My handle is too straight so the line
leads me to compensate. The cut is radical sustainability
in the overcode. If the blade
turns, shift the shoulders with it. Branch incursions
are just other books waiting to be written. The wood
is prime mover and the snap sound is the event
horizon of language.

the parking ticket

The idea of an absolute innocence, striped
sky motion and a memory of one meeting

that meant something. Space means this:
my poem and its time of reading, apart

from the curbs and blocks of ordered
trash, the rules of cash and transactional

English, how to work at a job, willingly
devoured or unnervingly dissected, taken

in, duped. So I stood, writing, and it wouldn't
matter except it does and will and the last

word standing is.

disfunctional title

growth by measurement, props
of entitlement improving on the last
quarter and what it might sink

vehicles tell us where to go
in the long run

skulls with clacking teeth, the whole
visual effect slouches across central street

the wrong alarms went off
and the volunteers never did make it

a better poet would miss this—
unpanicked lines more mellifluous

through us, fully enabled
nechako water moves

the making of the humans
would account for nothing
and find everyone

gas sniffing

the whole continent
bagged and burning
nostrils flared in danger

out back, exhaust pipe
lit by a low orange sun,
the boys lean on their pickups
and talk about girls

jobs across the mountains,
across those creatures made
numerical by distance, elevation,
the logistics of pipeline placement

the motorhand maintains the mud
pumps and seizes
the moment to smoke

for miles the plume
turns eyes: a show, a residue
an imprint dug up later
to tell us where we've been

for prince george citizens

                        close to
cottonwood siphons, travelled
in the blood valley and lakes
they stay where bills dissolve
and families of mergansers
reform from them

the air is a cipher;
the sidewalks crack with those already left

how a river might slice through
modernity as it outlasts its function—that affinity
to the sculptured moose with sunglasses,
the icons of too much beer,
northern hardware holding on

the welcome here—the pickup
pulls up exhausted holding the newspaper headline high:
the big men are coming to town tomorrow
and the streets are blocked with living

lettering on the old diner still in relief
proclaims that moss is filling our lungs
sucking out the beloved toxins without our knowing

you see, the going back is hardest, wheels
on the future paddle past the bank,
trust in disbelief and the way stones float

"tankful"

(& if they dare,
the system, the tangled boundary
(that has no place in what we learn as place)
deflates, at every encounter point

—George Stanley,
"Gentle Northern Summer"

1.
The Esso owner shoots me
a scowl when I ask, *You*
from around here? He is changing
the till and thinks I might rob him.
I consider

tracing the tributaries, the small
flow/large currency, where
the caches are, the upward
ascendancy of cash, torrents
from the station, 5th & Central,
to Vancouver, Calgary,
Toronto, New York, places

we go to
vacation, enjoy the amenities
(after all the fill-ups & hotel
expenses), the infrastructure
bought, at both ends,
by poor envious us

I would wish
not to be used

The gas plant chugs out
across the river, the local
thug & his territory—the truck
is god,
icon & driven.

2.
Back in the day,
the logs hauled by horse,
those men like the local grocer
bulldozed under by the 7-Eleven
on 20th (the VLA lives on Mars
bars) 18 wheels and the power
of conformity, all the

fast food and box stores smile,
give back to the community in charity,
overload the landfill.

If I bought in bulk,
would knowledge be cheaper?

We send raw logs, fire them
straight out to China
(me, little, trying to
dig there—like the trees)
& buy the kids meals
with plastic toys made in China
(the logs clog the system
in return) &

deflation occurs not at a point
of political catharsis

                      but upon the collapse,
the breaking point where nothing
is left, and we leave, get in the car
on empty.

thieves & preachers (fort george 1914)

The salmon-coloured mirror leans
closer, closer and then
smack into the forehead.

Don't mistake repulsion
for submissiveness, she crowed
from the back of a boat
heading north.

All this dog-garned country
is good for is growing Christmas trees
and trading posts for
modernity to land on;
fence-posts disguise the limit.

The Dreamland Theatre moved
on a sledge, the tickets
taken as ransom.

South & Central in the same tired drawl.

The site clear-cut for practice
the trees a nuisance even then;
how to get through not why, and
the lens trained to look back south.

Each southerner drawn
closer, closer and then
damned and darned
shut out by a strange voice
heading away, north.

the soft speakers (prince george 1741)

Traversed east-west the axis
of seasons a motion not a span. The rivers
then went around not through.
Less lush than overdone, the walkers
from there to there, when
here was somewhere. Back when
the traveller's track recorded
in hush and snare.

Imagined trails leading through
the poem, not from. The sentences
on the line cut
wide, overtaken as it
should be. Like parkland from
Grand Rapids through Saskatchewan
Rivers, then over. The living
was hard, a seasonal take.
The old tales moved. Still
do. Just not here.

wink books, inc.

over, there's the page where the language would have you
sold, secure; flipside, this is
the one that got away, fin flash

a story stalled long pauses and awkward
breaks enough to glimpse blur, flinch

the grain of wood, sawdust scent
flying up, the topography closer though,
felt in the roll of thighs, the eye-trained horizon, squint

after the speech, denial loaded into the back
a reverb stings the microphone; flipside, the subtext
twitches, an aside snuck, tucked

intimate meaning alongside the highways and
their agenda, a noise that rips the killed, rends

flipside; a book of herbs or ways of preserving
berries, fin and fat, paper-stained accidents and care, creased

i would give you this first from fort george before
the forest wars, or from after, a de-settling
pinch of paper and bone

II

poetry is dead

photo of crow

A gurgle ruffled from a morning
fog hunkered over the park, black
spruce float the sound higher
a sharp click and chuckle.

Lack of definition circles
the tallest evergreen, barks a tattoo
against the white air.

Myth a luminous absence—
the corrosive text, its toxic
sentence flowing out.

Poised here, an intersection of opportunity,
garbage, vantage, and disinterest, the possibility
of flight caught in a thick cracked beak and
a penultimate purple.

Poetry is dead, a photo
not taken, a scavenged plot
adapting itself to the wastelands.

waiting for winnipeg

not like a lover, a late
bus at main but
a slow progress of cumulous,
the air changed, your teeth singing
with the electric snap, expectation—

yes, that's it—a magnetic charge
across the valley not so much
a pull as a memory of depth,
lake bottom; the spits of lightning,
that (breathless) burst as the rain
comes, the air ripened, a ferment—
this all an attempt to submerge us again.

the elms would breathe then, swaying
kelp, their green revved, glowing
bark like the copper skin of kids
flashing, luminous and aquatic.

is it youth i am waiting for?

pedalling my bike by a girl's window
on one of those late summer nights
my wheel skidded on gravel and
i fell, my knee bursting open.

i remember at the time being tired
of this foolishness, wanting
to be older, articulate, able
to walk to the front door and
address desire.

i still wish this sometimes.

but winnipeg, that rain, the impossible
elms now all stand for that
young woman at her window
watching the wet boy pick himself up,

vow to write a poem.

did you say
for Fred Wah

(assembling what to say
remember the cajoling "don't *try* to say anything"

(the bumping of poetics
a shared space, a proximity,
an inevitable (joyous) commingling
(not know for sure (scree
but thinking
(identity, an uncut dish served
wham-bam between meals

so i ran to the other poet down the back alley   (of gorse
gave you the poem like it was my own

(i have a (eme mem) picture of you in
winnipeg after much wine nudging me into
the bc poetic landscape and you wished me
well; the guide teaches how to see
river snags not by pointing

(by not saying anything
knowing it would be   fixed

(a histology torqued
the slap-bang
fold between white and
pedagogy—a
beginning poetics of the alphabet's un
(hand in water

miki olson nichol bernstein stein silliman hejinian derksen
    marlatt mccaffery
(doing—a lack of pretense i suppose
(the *clinamen* he explained years   (toque in hand
sway and rupture—the habit
evacuation

(asking a lot of questions

(a sign waiting to be tipped
waiting for the fake home
freely knowing that, when it arrives,
we won't be sure

digging

like my father before
him the topsoil black,
seething with possibility;
i am not a farmer, neither
was he—the land wouldn't have us
haunted as it was

for the faintest suggestion
of shelter, a burrowing
through pine needle, nudging
star moss, paper lichen,
the morose corpse flower,

burrow down through loam
worm and braille tunnels
root networks slide aside
down to clay shelves and boulder fists
down to gneiss and granite slivered
with mica, shot through with
quartz, the bright memory of heat and
then *the present*, the molten arms,
chaotic embrace, the squalls and eddies of
stone in motion

we aren't miners either
but my father and i dig

down further, yes further
down to flesh;
an eyelid, a thigh

a restless sleep encircled
by dreams of corrosion, scars

I touch the mumbling lip
a hundred miles wide
the mountainous chin

Bly opens
his eye, wide
wild

the vasectomy
for Debbie

the split between subject
and object,   a releasing
of chance and the unplanned
fall of prepositions,   a gap
of love, indeterminate, concrete purple,

a way of knowing
history, its absences, the way
we forget,   just like that
the next word,   where
it goes

the message doesn't change, it skids
and frolics,   ambient in its delinquent delay
of please stay or don't go or am i   good enough
the message doesn't change, it fiddles
with the lock   tries on nylons

it just doesn't mean   as much anymore
click

the vasectomy 2

no violins and cellos
are out of the question

but ferns unfurl in creek beds
as the june sun lifts its paw

there is no time to turn back
time—should i have left that
door unlocked? did i leave
the stove on? could i have
become a singer?

i expected drama but all i got
was this poem

the baby nurses for hours
and we forget to bathe ourselves

like intimacy, it is a letting go

the vasectomy 3

to walk gingerly
after birth a right
of passage or umbilical
clamp you keep

a memento, a small
sound of bells and the grocer
asks how you are

down comforter or wobbling
knees i imagine it is
like a phone call from far away

you asking how i am
and when am i coming back

the traveller
for Justin

context versus direction, he
recognizes space less than a state
of shy consciousness with
just carry-on and no sharp objects

the boarding pass or thumb
is indistinct but officials let it
go knowing the threat is latent

monuments dissolve into a
conversation with one aboriginal
and the stories don't last long
but move the entire land

"things to do" list involves
nothing more and no collectibles
were secured

the return was by a different
route and whether he made
it is yet to be seen

loving seasons

he observes, desperately, the gravel road and evanescent
sky for signs of presence

absorb, embrace, consume
(fine spread this place)
a colonial occupation of the moment
perpetually hoping and nostalgia by
turns; the day flies by (roads
a washboard) the two pulls a kind of anguish
a theatrical death meant
for everyone

an intensity of perception held
taut, the linguistic sheen of
a smooth gun barrel

acuity he would call it later

the sky does not answer, "but
everything belongs to me, the lines
are clear, ambiguity belongs to the natives,
the riff-raff and here they come,
clamouring up the hill . . .

the first and last lines declare
the same thing, a syntax,
ownership shedding skin,
meaning self-evident, covenant

frailty mistaken as "love"—
"this beauty unasked for"

this trigger under cover, this scope,
this metallurgic insistence on my (that
presumption) presence

the vista leaves him standing there, the road,
the sky, his eyes, he stands
believing in the horizon, its commerce.

on pipes and linguistics

runnels of runoff ruins
a good gutter, syllables
slurred with slush & civic
pride, the purr of loaders
ticket-takers, the royal bank
building grate the cleanest of all

i study sewers, culvert
covers, the out-of-the-way
drains into the river i swim
in the waste, taste its
briney blush, its foamy
black, its slick rainbow flavours

my fists drive deep into drifts
of landfills, dumpsters,
the deep unthought caught
in my hands, between curbs,
jobs, the exhaust of a tired way of being

a death grip with the real

the mill smells (the spirits
of dead carrier dead salmon)
a halo fat against my being
my flesh—*denial*, a word in english
spoken without a tongue

cancers collect on my skin, a tattoo
of rashes, tumours of love

i inhale downwind, a cigarette
filter by the pub entrance,
an assemblage of particulates,
the stone masonry dissolving in sweat

this beautiful death, a pristine
undoing, my art
lasts just that instant longer

ornithographical imprints

1.
a feathered awning
the idea of a bird, en-
circling a sun, any sun—
a muslin pact between light
and ascension

eyelids become envious
of that flutter, that
dart into shadow, that
utterly benign illusion

dispelled

eyes lower

2.
a feathered awning
the idea of a bird, en-
blazoned, stylized
insignia shot through with meaning,
    history, ritual, machine

and the man-made manuals to work it,
collude in the abstract symbol—

a clean, clean window

3.
the furtive hops and swoops
of the flesh (whisper)
of impossible mid-
air insights, hollow bones,
incantations of breeze

how like the subtle shifts of plot

landing, wings closed

4.
a lone junko calls it serendipity
clearly, before the worldly sun denies everything
(a faltering belief in non-production), palimpsest even,
the colours once used in a painting
(plastics, chemically produced dyes, poison compounds),
holding the eye, the colour holding the
idea holding the eye holding
an empty winged shape,
an empty shape
emptied

(there will be snow soon)

5.
and so arranging the taxidermist's arms
propped over the wing arch of a grouse,
enfolding the shape in a awkward embrace
(translated as *realism=sales*)
whose outline serves as a surface sketch of *use*,

the wooden base, the wire frame, the glass eyes,
a lost trust, all these defenses of fear compose
the terror of the taxidermist's art,
the humming beak inches from his trembling eye

6.
the eagle turned (a
crossing) into myth, turned
into hauntings turned (a
tossing) into sleep, turned
into motion, flight (a
way)

7.
bought an "Indian-painted" feather at a tourist stop
the "Pioneer Village" gift shop

(nesting doubt)

8.
my daughter caught the nest, its fall
an arc across constructions of eden,
or epiphany,
her four years of age stationing her hand
just so, the blue eggs, the robin's eggs.
the fragile burst of thought caught
on her face

the nest dislodged from sameness

the eggs becoming

9.
a magpie caught in the rafters,
the foundations of our mortality

10.
she sees unborn souls in the suspended
hummingbird's gaze like the sound of surf in seashells

it's eyeing the sunflower on her t-shirt, humming
a siren-song to lure her naked into the woods

the seduction is subtle and she
gathers flowers to sew into shawls, sashes,
the silences between words

she licks the edge of lilies as she passes

11.
a pair of whisky jacks check us out,
the thieving resistance of plain luck

the soup

make it quickly, without
speaking and use only what's
at hand, chance is your ally
the pot, the colander without rim

—don't drive anywhere,
ever, walk, write, or invite a neighbour
with the ingredients, never go
for flash or imports—keep it local,
simple, smell the bunch and you'll know

it should be chilly outside but
no flurries yet; the words
diffuse ice fog, a suggestion of
spice but let the stock take it all

toss it together the timing and
root and juices and let it stew

tell a friend what's in it and
how poetry is hearty, how
it cleans the blood

there should be no flourish or garnish
no main dish or dessert;
don't let one vegetable dominate the dish—
variety is the strength, what keeps it going

the ladle and bowl should be plain,
well made and sturdy, it will

be scuffed and nicked with use—
this is a good sign

serve hot so it fills the room with its
energy, be assured it is a mantra, something
to believe in, something you're part of

the poetry cops

a flap jacket pose a billy
club delivery a badge
flash search warrant posse
thoughts rifle the world a radar
speed trap a plastic strap
breathalyzer slammed against
the car spread eagle cherries spinning and then

the poetry reading ended

a long sentence for those uninitiated
to the art of colonizing language

you have the right to remain

security cameras on the premises
the covert lyric slices
malls and rivets the sky
spies on the sly
excesses of the outsiders

juiced up on perception he loves
himself looking and that facility
with language oh so
eloquently flies into flesh

please stand up for the court

a taser to the tongue to numb
and incapacitate the other class

but the law slumbers night
poetry spills and swaps
pills and pleases the unanchored
drift of this nonpersistent riff
a pop-off flighty thing
a tweak and finagle of lines
drunk down

curiouser

for George Bowering

Not that it means anything. The name, I mean. *Part* of a larger book that, on its own, doesn't amount to much. Or perhaps a synonym for gallantry: to "bowering" into a room larger than life. Or the book.

He says politicians with a pah—like spitting snuff—and pisses on the Peace Tower lawn. Larger than life. They want him to memorialize them in poetry. They say poetry with an odd colonial inflection that makes him want to spit. A counterpoint to the bells, ta da tum.

He wrote Vancouver from its sleep while in Greece. Or is that Greece from its sleep in Vancouver. Or did he visit with Kroetsch there. All the same. The game, I mean.

Baseball sucks. And it's American. There, I said it. Bowering'd be proud of my guts and he's gonna kick the shit out of me too. Might as well say the Red Sox got lucky.

Trying not to be obnoxious, he succeeds. A flourish of bowering. A gregarious lifetime of bowering to the ladies. Ta da tum. The name, I mean. An extravagant bowering, bared chest love, a reading like a courting song. Courtly bowering.

He's the horse-sweat and muscle in the urbane. A poet's economy laid bare: the lower mainland's interior, the cariboo in false creek, shit backwards. The name, I mean.

He's really a Prince George poet you know and he could be my prime mover, my administrator (in names). Used to be poets had to be flakey; nowadays they're tough like jerky, knock you spinning soon as look at you. Wiry and gallant. He can piss on the public lawns in my country any day. And it would mean something.

a wakened image

a mother raccoon lies
on the side of the road

her back leg is stretched
out, like she was running
in her dreams, her fine paw
splayed, relaxed

her front paw is draped
over her ear
not wanting to hear

     i know
if i were to stop the car
get out (a warning ringing bing bing bing)
and walk back she would continue
to feign sleep, chuckling inwardly
knowing my attention
would be diverted

kits tucked away in the wild rose bush
a stone's throw from the road

a sly one that mother raccoon, lying
there for so long, the flies
almost making her twitch—

my friend the feminist

for Si Transken

a real push this
the whispers a loud curtain
tailed asps and leer

petal and pedals the gears
locks and spade—oppression
is a spectator sporting
a tweed jacket backing out
laws to paint the scene over
    a corrosive residue

a real fish this
water we live in

my friend the feminist and
I am sometimes there
swimming against the whispers

walking out of the toxins
a motion the same and together
when separation is art and blur the tool

tay creek

Into Stuart, into town, in
quietude the water means more

banality. Closer to the ground, walking stride made
a greening of my way. A kind of stopping.

The car sits unperturbed, waiting completion
of rust. Thinking about people and

machines and writing. Here, the machine is still.
The writing runs on water, trust, leafy greens, berries

from around here. I am
from around, here is a place mimicking another

story, one further out toward the centre of
language. Ken knows the way. The streets

swim with fish, follow us home.

represent

Being carried along, far
past what I was
going to say:
past 100 Mile House and
the push of the placed poem
tells me this.

The search might not look
pretty but it cleans the system
after spring runoff, the sand and salt
gone; puts the present under way,
to think again as an understudy,
here, as if dying.

Here, virtual wealth smells
fear, the forest den shakes out
rage into migration—
what is left never existed you see,
and walks back into town.

A system snaps back into place like teeth.
Roots let loose without loss.

Another form could be filled out-
side the allotted space, the word
"bush" repeated as if it was.

Don't ask about budgets, the paper
won't mind. Working at bark, at walking
out, diverging the way before it leaves.

the line
for Ken Belford

not even catch and release, more release and release the line
less harassing more play a barbless watching over the river

just a hint of a hook he said slyly
to pull them out, think twice

i remember you by that willow overhang
the steelhead replied slyly, and the poem is just starting

the streets move, dump truck plume or fleet
bicycle jump—where do you wait for the fish?

depth, temperature, season, family
what you leave behind, how you relate, send forth

slow, deliberate, not like fences but paths
the river topography traversed with waiting

the cast recognized by the guide who's
jigging a syntax, ah, here we go again, river-
bottom trails and hey, here comes ken.

foley's cache

for Jeremy

At a time when authenticity
was never a question, he was

the outfitter, the rest stop
on the journey to

fame. Fortunate horses
watered and a shot of

whiskey to ease the saddle
sores. The cache a stash

clinging to the river
way north. It turns though

the current, the cash twists
in the watershed. Those going

up, bright streaks of
miles, media metal ringing

in their fingers. Those
going down, broken

wheels looking for anything
to keep their horse

alive. I wait by the
storehouse, cataloguing

the provisions out: oatmeal, salt,
sugar, canned meat, a satchel

of self.

the universe

I am the academic inside out. I am there.
Can't say I'd miss the organization or its
mandates—that's not where it's at. I eat well
and my heart is in the way of everything I do.
I can spend a day on one word. Work is an act

of discovery—if it's not, it's something else.
I bring gumption and disorder into meetings and
I often leave early. I ride the system like a bus
to reduce emissions. I am an american but working
it out. Like poisons in sweat. Poets are my historians and

politicians and I am healthier because of it. I am an email
gamesman, a roll-out passer, a bank-shot they didn't see
coming. The structure is not structural, it is home-
grown and out of sync with the ghosts of real
knowing, like the street. It's not what it is but what it does

to you. Footwork, not fancy but dodgy. The administration
is confused by gifts and making a difference, differentiating
study and feeling. I feel the halls releasing, failing to
complete themselves. I am there. Others too, disowned
but drifting back in, taking up
the slack, what's let go for bigger

prizes. The money talks, gags. The show
is fragile. Public relations is out of style; I can't hear it any
more. Hyphens striate the offices. I drift
in. Out. Back in. If I ever
become an academic, I will do so sure that it doesn't
mean anything. Then the building will be complete.

how to be here too
The Form quivers in the deer

–Tim Lilburn

and where are you
exactly? the word's vibration
imprecise like sights or punctuality, the written land
    isn't one or multiple or uncertain—
like a theory of water,
one doesn't pre-exist the other
except here, where you are
thirsty, difficult

"nature" doesn't write
back

a muscle-like simile composed in the bush
is hunting, tireless; a label tagged
to each part of the pastoral
law

what is taken out of the land is a softcover
book you've been meaning to
but forgotten and tried to sing instead—it turned out
badly and the lies and
gasoline keep spilling

III

chemical enhancement

modernity

all of it made carefully, overtop
the ground, calculations of amplitude,
erosion, gestation;

the engineers looked over their shoulders
down and away, a blueprint of forgetting

fingertips placed gently together in front
of the magistrate's words

it is not mortality i am fighting;
it is what that sure-footed vision gets you
that bothers me

the coherence cannot hold

power grids, establishment
reckoning, the aesthetics taught as formative—
all those attempts to justify
the expenditure, the waste, the damage ...

it is a letting go, an un-named
un-naming strolling over the hill
i seek   no longer
god or mystery
but the anonymous among us

strange meat

it is not so much the unfamiliarity—
the texture is the same every time—
as the idea that you too might be farmed
in small stalls, no light, overgrown
with chemicals to enhance
how well you wrote platitudes of
nature poetry about the forest
you've never seen

like work or actual
community, vegetables ground
the earth and you in it

the strange meats on the table
grow wings and art
takes it to books as the truth

like white bread and big
sugar, the factory lines
of industry and long hooks
clog the anthologies

disbelieving strawberries

You can't, they aren't
anymore (unless by accident);
denial tumbled into the cart,
the monster rising from the table ...

These they burgeon
an addict's needle
sprayed by profit and regulated
labour like a cancer on desiccated fields
the malathion a pall over humus ...

By the side of the side under trespassing leaves
unless surprised by taste we
stopped shopping,
looked around ...

power outages:
    walking back to the river today

mortality swung on streetlights flicker
awake, addicts looking
two for one specials and scarves
fall, collect the taxes, nutrients

lovers leak into sports events, hair
salons, the payphone at mr. g

catalysts for gold left looking
and the sky wonders at power
outages, the ingredients in shampoo

gateways are easy endings on the fifth
floor, stories have trouble skating
during that first cold snap, cable is
too expensive, an old woman dies
of too much CNN and wonder bread

the rivers don't care, push through
like highways or oilrig workers like
too much cash, burnt hands, windshield glass
scattered leaflets, the walkways lined
with saskatoons nobody eats

another mr. noodle overcooked

an angel appears to twelve people on
brunswick, near the tracks;

he says we work too hard
fiddles with his snow-white belly

a meeting ends at the college,
nothing was decided

fifteen minutes until the news

twenty-two hours until she leaves for vancouver

* * *

3:42 p.m. Tuesday, January 20   Prince George

an act of rediscovery
every time the red light
breaks, the cop swings his arm to oncoming
violence, the pepper spray smell
of queensway

on monday, without warning
the bridges disappeared.
pigeons were inconsolable,
commuters hung out at the gas stations,
saw the mid-morning light grow

* * *

5:56 p.m. Tuesday, January 20   Prince George

that pink ruff
you know
sends water

haida gwaii tipping
her hat, grinning

the other way, robson is singing alto tenor
a hurting song like brooks & dunn

lonesome lonesome

the weather does matter
and you are here

          ✱   ✱   ✱

6:41 p.m. Tuesday, January 20   *Prince George*

cottonwood dream

deluge, the end of mandibles

rot, leavings

more sky more

earthsigns turning

the entitlement

always been there, latent bones
of self-evident poems
knowing just where to go
how much it costs
what resources are waiting there

in the memory of a land
management office, with the chair
placed a power position mantle
credentials or dream charm and off to the next task
walking in seemly

stock options are mandatory
and run of the mill

older men strut in, carry their weight
with trim haircuts and
plastic in their pocket embossed
with who fucked who and how fast
the truck is fucking too

the title is full, foremost,
bucolic and tells the whole

vulgar and effective, the force
carries with it residues of meanness—
chaos as torture to induce compliance

just mildew on words but
a catalyst for the stylist's cover;
geographies rolled in smoke

the plant that grows at white men's doors

peevish and sallow
those vehicles of free range
fences and false
fronts, the business of skins,
carcasses carrying people away

chilcotin ranches shit
by degrees the river rises
eggs fry

space translated into place by
names, the plants, the ones noticed anyway

trains derail, and the lake name becomes toxic,
but all our wells are connected you know

the territory created by routes through
or routes disallowed; what century do you travel in?

most of the lakes remain over the hill though,
not waiting for tailings to swallow,
but sensing a change in the air
like the sound of infinite beehives
from the south, blooming up, burning out

colonial traces take root, spread over
meadows in a brilliant malignancy—
the names of these are fitfully recorded
for future recovery

the myth of forestry runs deep,
channels down hillsides,
ends up back in vancouver

the plant smells off, sickly,
withstands the boots of second thoughts,
third spaces of the land

nass talking

across the valley it would be
before confederation before
colonization, you and I and all
drums and poetry retro a kind
of coming home differently

blade handles and bridges and ideas closer
at hand, fitted green
not assembled
expanding into place

skeena nass nechako fraser
peace it would have to be
bound together by water—voices
unencoded to float

hear me when i say such a time
never happened

it would have to be a season
undetermined and when i called
animals would hear and know as always

across a valley still tracked by
colonial leavings—partaken,
the work of detox abating—
the shot healed
a gradual decommissioning of beef
and turning lanes

it would have to be easy, a shout
cajoling leisure out of the day

it would have to be uncertain what i
was saying in the weather or not

incorrigible and forgiving
you might hear or not and
across the valley what matters

limbic ghosting

the one unindexed, an assumption
of the grammatical,
florid in its inbetweenness and
candour, tending to lurch, crass counter-
productive and sweet

meetings in the green
belt—such languish
on a coast and inward
rivers coursing into books

the present no
presence at all—a flash
of syntax sought, turned
into fingers, tossed

into writing before the sentence
sentinel happens to clear it up, usable
and serene
retinal trace

re-potting interpretation

1.
the curvaceous word a
cyclamen petal bending
stem and the absence
of scent—a passage of colour or
the sound of surprise over
salmon-pink, the pause of hyphen
between readings, this thing-
ness so close and yet
impossible

2.
starry sky inverted bright
green the moss overtakes
me, deprives reference

a mind a stony cliff-
face agog with wetness
hardly holding onto
the page and gravity

3.
a seed that isn't,
sterile, benign but
each poem a non-
starter, a stony kernel
and its promise

4.
and what is it about *form*
that makes me keep trying

5.
success depending on moisture
a newness a primordial swirl
we all imagine a magic
conjuration or miracle vast
as a planet

but the dirt smells sweaty,
work, an organic stew—
a measure,
this is all that's here

6.
but the original sits
a lump of knotted roots
and i pick it up
like the old poets showed me
lean over and tear away at the cosmic gnarl
loosen the ends, send
them into directions
break up hard-packed
intention locked in place

doctrine, habit
tumble onto the floor

7.
ideas the runners falling over the lip
window to forest and untimely deaths—
or they root in the deep recesses,
the ravines of other mouths

the regional materialist

can't be when there and here
is a bias of communication, a trick
of the wind patterns or
myths that have forgotten what they are

they asked me for ID
and i said your poems
desecrate graves with
their assurance

i see cutting the lawn as
a way to let only imported
grasses survive except
at the edges

i am a type of trying to
do too much but what's
the difference between status
quo work and the police state
poetics of look at me

it is a commitment to not
and the writing lines bend
to hold that evasion:
look, there it goes

tumble light: studying the photo's punctum
Tumbler Ridge 2002

uses of the particular, past
the redundancy of words

we are moved, moving

it is who we are

sex in retrospect, BC
for Barry

not what you'd expect   looking back
togetherness a skewed article
oddly placed conjunction and
clothing—the economy of closets

     *   *   *

like a sentence
memory and prediction conspiring
the rules and the mis
     spoken times the first/
     best/last accidents of the body   (passion?
in a warm van preposition in any season
fort george park—earliest settlement
     and Lheidli T'enneh graveyard love is erasure against

     *   *   *

prince george embraces
     the rest, the has-been, the stalwart, the strangely
     erotic a matter of downtown revitalization

my street with kids
first time in years
they're my kids and
they look around for more

college heights a high
social measure—the price,
the highway disbelieving

who screws who

* * *

come on, you're romanticizing
          –BX pub, 2001

* * *

like chapbooks
          doing it yourself in your own basement
like a reading at mosquito
          just inebriated enough
like a university meeting
          late and involving assholes
like a caravan in winter
          no control and broken down (only as good as
like your tired bones

* * *

fragments of a life
assembled sexuality a cumulative
hope—like desire—receding nechako ice
     rivulets caught, bright oily

* * *

come on

* * *

lokanathan calls caledonia
down, her rough lips breaking

skin—mind the beer bottle
bard at night—a logging truck
rumbling through your thighs

industrial climax, a smoke
ah, *the smell of money*

＊ ＊ ＊

start again   this time

＊ ＊ ＊

muggings and decades-old vomit
the care it takes to stay
thirty-five years, to stay
until the feeling arrives, to stay
home despite

the awkward *tawdriness* of it all, skills
at scouring pawnshops

＊ ＊ ＊

men talking over beer about
health issues, diet—the vulnerable words
a gentle calibration w/out doctors;
what should we do? what's the name
of that salve again?

＊ ＊ ＊

patricia is a street and

a stripper   which

     ❋   ❋   ❋

sex at this time is a place
is knowing that 3rd st. turns
into 5th st. and what that perspective takes
away and holds closer

prince rupert (chatham sounds)

subject/object with a shoreline
about it

(the weather: fog people
moving through the shroud
anticipating the metaphors
for language dissipating)

seaweed eelgrass the wood
silver and the sky hardly

(the sonics of paddlestroke
the seals know
as space)

mountain is to passage
as coast is to horizon although
not in the context of raven
and canneries

(call a stone thrown green-gold
from a great height how
awake are you and is
the cliff-face made of dynamite)

Tsimshian ground the story is
here like a turned eye and
sidelong gaze from a watery
rheumy glance

(the sea otter's pelt
gone—the scent of a place's sinew)

that sound at the back of the throat
I am not able imaginatively

(what was migration
now a vagrancy)

this is what happens
when you learn history from poets

(a people in gillnets
complete families—the coho
ask a question)

when a whole town is a call
centre waiting to downsize
move on

(perhaps we are still in an immense potlatch)

the country broods the city
and the third, belford's mountains
and maybe a fourth, the coast
its waters pacing occupation differently

(the mall faces out to sea;
happy shopping reveals
the end in expenditure)

development spills into the sound
from pipes; the halibut scarce and

the cruise ships dump shit
tourists on thursdays, leave
on thursdays with the grand
Empire painted over on its bow and
the horn is too loud ...

(scenic is not what it seems)

cruise

"norwegian dream" or some dis-
placement carried over the escape
a package of metal floating over the inlet

Tony Blair calls on Londoners to *go on*
with their business—to be afraid
is to let the terrorists win   the tracks
cleared, the schedule resumed

what it means to truly disembark
the infamous missile, remote
controlled, the target a fuzzy
bunker filled with crosshairs

the permanent tourist stands in front
of the monument, history then
a digital file emailed to oneself

the horn sounds announcing
what? you too can dive into
a swimming pool on the Pacific
and become weightless

at the crest, prince rupert

cursing small dogs and
their owners who leave them locked in cars
barking against upholstery—
it's never enough

i am in my underwear reading
Purdy poems ("At the Quinte Hotel"
now and yes, *poems will not really buy beer*)
watching bad US TV (the war movie
on mute, the hero dying for nothing
not a goddamn thing)

here, where poetry and place are conditional;
the weather and my walks
miss everything

the beams of the museum are whole trees
and the importance of this is lost

at the pub there are no yellow flowers;
instead the Tsimshian laws break and there is nothing
left but pan-pacific business and chain stores

the harbour, the train, the beginning
word—awareness—at the verge and
the sockeye and halibut
decline without elegies, because
of elegies

(water still moves and
i hope to be swept out)

back on land, the space muscles itself
aside (my place in economic
indicators), the rain continues unabated,
the pretense of "civilization"
floats here

the mine fields

Going under and pulling it up—
when the first venture fails
the surface face wasted
the smart politician knows
how to sling theoretical mud.

Forgone, water sluiced through
loaded with displacement psychology,

the shaft is hard and deep
and barely contained in
the conference room projector.

The ministry requires the view
to stay the same exposure,
the text a neutral tint
of traditional. What it means,
a headline.

Jobs are plain prose and
economies male. Writing
suffers the mercury, doesn't
survive the relocation because
of the new ph levels. Roads
cut arts funding and
leave the land for
maps to devour.

The open field of reading
closed to all but trucks
carrying money to feed

the headwaters to the wolves
or, worse, the TSX.

So the meeting doors shut
out the snout's quiver, consultation a
chemical slough, drainage and tailings
are means and news
releases into the upturned faces
with glee. A quick visit
by the premier, photos
cut, tape snapped, words
reportedly taken.

The mess begins months ago,
on target, before the market
shifts the plateau and the dolly varden
flips into the real desert.

rehab central

for Dr. Barry McKinnon, honoris cavillatio

missing or might as well, the limbic memory
a wound, a beautiful whorl, the crescents
of skin where we saw
it once before

the shock of arrival stuns us, the nerves
peeled back, the ghosts of the first,
people on the street an original
dislocation

and the blades keep falling
and the forest
wars go on

healing bulldozers, their tracks
burn, pick up the rivers who doze
by the bank, losing interest
like people, and transfer toxins
from place to place

standing on the silence of the cutbank
wondering what consciousness
was sheered away

    left and leaving
    the place on the way
    to somewhere else—but
    it is here contact is made,
    the city a product of friction here

a healing, a replacing
the habitation, the transience of this marginal
city and its valley—
a watery stillness so quick it loses us

subject & object

1.
the prose time-
span overloaded with causation, as if
one opposes one grammatically

the verb looks both ways, retreats
both ways

2.
the conjunction of two rivers, say
nechako and fraser (it is calm, yellow, a mild
morning and the person standing on the shore-
line taking notes is one or the other) the flow
is unfixed except directionally
and even then to
what end and how long

3.
reading writing or writing
to: a placement, a laying
on of hands

4.
of love, one inquires

of certainty, one (and the other gestures
of language, pronouns fail

of pronouns, one wonders at the structure

of structure, one hopes there is more, or less

of hopes, one requires great feelings

of love

5.
the way syntax might decide
the next part of speech or dissemble
saying next next next next the extenuating
way syntax might decide
repeatability turned on itself over-
loaded with causation aware
of itself turned over
the way syntax might
or dissemble

6.
upon arrival i (the subject) was
unaware of the history of the place
(the object) called Prince George; i,
upon arrival began to research
(the verb) the history (the verb)
and write (the verb); i,
Prince George, and verbs of
being

7.
upon arrival i reconsidered
my subject (position) and my object
(perception (verb))

for example: Jack Spicer lives here

a kind of counter-history
(you see what i mean)
circling like a verb
looking both ways

8.
the fiction opposed grammatically
but not across from, the shore-
lines wavering across time,
the movement alluvial, cut-
banks rising and falling, trees
rising and fallers passing, the friction
of passing over the place
and between
one and
one passing, a strained
grammar of being

IV

the untrained eye

the untrained eye
who carries me
so secretly

—Fred Wah, "My Horse"

1.
the impossible train track
imagined by the route

me, then, rerouted through
iron, stone, stream

the tracks diverging
mine being one

2.
the window moves
the line along

and then the other
side, lighter, open

the train and its
twinned vision

3.
a rhythm undone
the stops erratic

words flash, some
caught some not
and arrival sits still—
thinking *here, here, here* ...

4.
overly constructed, ordered
to measure the passage

the schedule escapes
the timetable waves

back, paper stirring in
signs, horns, watching

5.
"a lake called syntax"
or glacier locked

fossil or echo echoing
the station an apparition

i thought it was
you, your voice

6.
named, renamed, the
authorities forgiving, pleased

brochures toward meaning
the places are reread
a route west closed
to the illiterate ocean

7.
via rail tickets
lost or purchased

a railing against
almost frictionless space

an idea tumbling
in the baggage car

8.
the story set
in stages, causes

a to *b* the points
a purpose, momentum

in the in-between:
waving to the particles

9.
a doing over
and overly robust

do the job,
conduct the way

traveling over land
landing the view

10.
water drops on
window, the window

wet, clear with
rain and light

the sun intermittent
spraying against this

11.
pencil neck they
called me on

the trip, writing
itself back and forth

across the window
noticing this and that

12.
the untrained eye
off course, awry

commenting on the
mundane, unhistoric

politics of food
and where we're going

13.
mile signs run
up and down

to zero, and
up again, hope

measured not against
language, but syntax

14.
one passenger passed
out woke everyone

with a start
where are we?

as if the collective
could change our reply

15.
when too much
cramped into seats

is too much
of everything, miles

traversed for nothing
or smaller thoughts

16.
built for epics
the frontier, all

the stories piled
into efficient cars

and the next
episode disembarking now

17.
writing joggled a
turn by the river

bend and off
kilter, the lean

measured to prevent
derailing, or ambiguity

18.
the sound could
be imitated, a kind

of onomatopoeia placed
deliberately, a realism

to trick the reader
into being here

19.
the septic sucking
truck rolled up

we were full;
when words fill

the page, they
are easily missed

20.
sigh, the compartment's conversation
inane and erratic

ailments and a child's
drawing passed around

a collective breath
a planet of air

21.
one ellipses after
another question of

what comes next;
the connecting pauses

to wait out form—
the connection, the switches

22.
hb pencil and
eraser, traveling length-wise

the mark appearing,
disappearing, reading carefully

and forgetting;
the land stays

23.
a curved bridge
across a swift current

a slow climb
up and eroding mountain

a line of writing
in northern bc

24.
i rode the train
every summer

the train ran
all year round

the winter listened
for the q sounding

25.
i read the train
ride the book's

spine, the train
cracks open

unfurled, the text
flies by

26.
when thought
on the thing

impinges, a scar
of gravel, iron

or passes with
a bow, wave

27.
window the size
of a torso

a stone's throw
from the nechako

the shock of
lungs considering this

28.
houston, hazelton, burns
lake, the way

settled decades recorded
as displacement—

the train hits
the land again

29.
skeena, bulkley, nechako
flow off the head

the waters of
poetry coursing

three ways:
original, settled, imaginary

30.
the nation of
the imagination

with no representations;
a kind of law-

-lessness where we
know the other

31.
queen and colonial
construct—the sounding

at crossings;
the imprint

a ritual safety
measure for effect

32.
watershed and economics,
tributaries to the larger

idea; the ideal
leaving, living

by the water
shed, dispersing

33.
bc rail, the public
disowned, wondering

the line crossed,
the motives weighed

how will we
find our way?

34.
near mcbride
horses by the tracks

think of kroetsch's
studhorse, the cover and

what their similarities
are opposed to

35.
six seats back
the poem's ending

arrives in a
whispered confession

maybe i should do
something, besides watch

36.
poplar bark peeling
slow wet roll

thumb against blade
balanced against blood

a laying bare
the shore line

37.
second growth
invader species

the railroad
clearing sway

by degrees
and scale

38.
a laying bare;
the poetic line

the exposed root,
a scree slide—

spare rock face
uncertain what it means

acknowledgements

The number of people who have influenced this text about equals the population of Prince George. Some, though, have been essential to literary culture in Prince George, crucially present in the process of writing this, or have lent direct editing and advising help with the manuscript: Ken Belford, Barry McKinnon, George Stanley, Greg Lainsbury, Si Transken, the Second Words Workshop group, Jeremy Stewart, Justin Foster, Denielle Wiebe, Carly Stewart, Michael Latala, Richard Krueger, Derrick Denholm, Graham Pearce, Michael Cruickshank, Adam Pottle, "hardy," rob mclennan, Jay MillAr, Jim Brinkman, Dee Horne, Heather Larson, Simon Thompson, Alisa Thompson, Heather Glasgow, Earson Gibson, Paul Strickland, Al Rempel and Gillian Wigmore. Other writing influences are written into the poems so I won't repeat them here, except to say thank you, all, for the poems. I'd also like to recognize the support of UNBC and the UNBC English Program in my creative work and the institution's growing commitment to the arts in Northern BC. Thank you to Silas White for his dedicated and careful editing work. Finally, thank you to my family for dealing with the distracted state of mind the activity of finding Ft. George takes.

Individual poems in the book have been previously published in *George Street Letters*, *Jacket*, *It's Still Winter/ Treeline*, and *Prairie Fire*.

ROB BUDDE teaches Creative Writing and Critical Theory at the University of Northern BC in Prince George. He has previously published five books (two poetry collections—*Catch as Catch* and *traffick*, two novels—*Misshapen* and *The Dying Poem*, and most recently short fiction—*Flicker*). In 2002, Rob facilitated a collection of interviews, *In Muddy Water: Conversations with 11 Poets*.